tools of the **believer**

tools of the believer

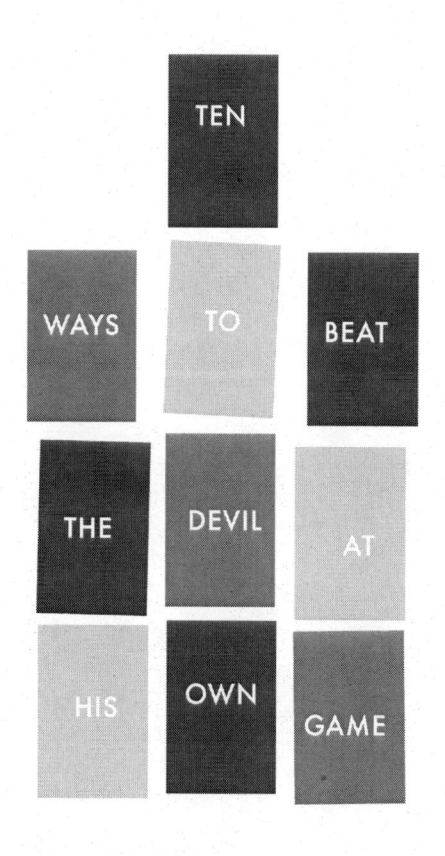

TEN WAYS TO BEAT THE DEVIL AT HIS OWN GAME

BY MINISTER CHERYL JEFFRIES

TATE PUBLISHING
& Enterprises

Tate Publishing is committed to excellence in the publishing industry. Our staff of highly trained professionals, including editors, graphic designers, and marketing personnel, work together to produce the very finest books available. The company reflects the philosophy established by the founders, based on Psalms 68:11,

"THE LORD GAVE THE WORD AND GREAT WAS THE COMPANY OF THOSE WHO PUBLISHED IT."

If you would like further information, please contact us:
1.888.361.9473 | www.tatepublishing.com
TATE PUBLISHING & *Enterprises*, LLC | 127 E. Trade Center Terrace
Mustang, Oklahoma 73064 USA

Tools of the Believer: 10 Ways to Beat the Devil at His Own Game
Copyright © 2007 by Cheryl Jeffries. All rights reserved.
This title is also available as a Tate Out Loud product.
Visit www.tatepublishing.com for more information

No part of this publication may be reproduced, stored in a retrieval system or transmitted in any way by any means, electronic, mechanical, photocopy, recording or otherwise without the prior permission of the author except as provided by USA copyright law.

All scripture quotations are taken from the Holy Bible, King James Version, Cambridge, 1769. Used by permission. All rights reserved.

The opinions expressed by the author are not necessarily those of Tate Publishing, LLC.

Book design copyright © 2007 by Tate Publishing, LLC. All rights reserved.
Cover design by Leah LeFlore
Interior design by Lynly D. Taylor

Published in the United States of America

ISBN: 978-1-6024733-3-1

07.04.10

This book is dedicated to my "Paul," Dr. Joseph Butler Sanders Parks, Pastor of Greater Grace Community Baptist Church, Winston-Salem, NC.

Acknowledgment

Daily, I thank God for my Boaz, my prince charming, the love of my life, a man I cherish and adore, my husband, Rufus Christopher Jeffries, a man who possesses the patience of Job when it comes to his wife. I thank him for spending countless hours with me as I ponder and prepare sermons, for studying God's Word with me, for having a listening ear, for always supporting and encouraging me, for accepting me for who I am, for loving me unconditionally, for making my dream possible…

Without him, this book would not be…

Preface

Trying to survive this great game of life
Full of trouble and woe, difficulty and strife
The game isn't over until I win
I'll play it over and over again
Often finding myself fleeing from sin
The opponent is sneaky, tricky and devious
Out to steal, kill and even deceive us
He likes to fight morning, noon and night
No half-stepping, using all his might
I now realize that I can beat him
I don't have to run, hide or be a victim
For I've learned the rules of the game
Nothing new he tries; it's all the same
Indeed we know it's truly all in vain
10 ways to beat him at his own game
Of this book is the purpose, the goal, and the aim!

Introduction

Taking an Offensive Approach

What is our position? Do we find ourselves on the offense or the defense? We know that the opponent is the devil, and many times we find ourselves on the defense as the devil is seeking whom he may devour. We need to turn it around on him and be on the offense.

It is time for us to stop being on the defensive and take an offensive approach, for God has given us authority and power over the enemy! "Then he called his twelve disciples together, and gave them power and authority over all devils, and to cure diseases" (Luke 9:1).

In sports, the offense has possession of the ball. The offense is trying to score. Indeed, it is time that we, as Christians, take an offensive approach. The enemy is increasing his advances, and we cannot continue to sit idly by, attempting to defend ourselves.

Certainly, we know that the devil was defeated, even at the cross. "And having spoiled principalities and powers, he made a show of them openly, triumphing over them in it" (Colossians 2:15). In time, the devil will indeed receive his due (Revelation 20). Until that time, when he is cast into the lake of fire and brimstone, he does all that he can, attempting to wreak havoc in our lives. Hence, we must take an offensive approach and be equipped at beating the devil at his own destructive game. We can prevent and hinder the enemy by ensuring that we are equipped, that we are utilizing the tools that God has given us as believers.

> **The enemy is increasing his advances, and we cannot continue to sit idly by, attempting to defend ourselves.**

"For though we walk in the flesh, we do not war after the flesh: (For the weapons of our warfare are not carnal, but mighty through God to the pulling down of strongholds;)" (II Corinthians 10:3–4).

What is the devil's game?

Job 1:7 "And the Lord said unto Satan, Whence comest thou? Then Satan answered the Lord, and said, From going to and fro in the earth, and from walking up and down in it."

I Peter 5:8 "Be sober, be vigilant; because your adversary the devil, as a roaring lion, walketh about, seeking whom he may devour."

John 10:10 "The thief cometh not, but for to steal, and to kill, and to destroy…"

As the aforementioned scriptures indicate, the devil's game is clear, for he is going to and fro, walking up and down in the earth, as a roaring lion, seeking whom he may devour, seeking to steal, kill, and destroy.

As Christians, we are looking forward to that day when we will be with our heavenly Father.

In Revelation 21: 1–3, it states:

¹And I saw a new heaven and a new earth: for the first heaven and the first earth were passed away; and there was no more sea.

²And I John saw the holy city, new Jerusalem, coming down from God out of heaven, prepared as a bride adorned for her husband.

³And I heard a great voice out of heaven saying, Behold, the tabernacle of God is with men, and he will dwell with them, and they shall be his people, and God himself shall be with them, and be their God.

Until that day, we seek to fulfill the God-given purpose for which we were placed here on earth. The devil's game is to prevent us from reaching the goal. He does not want us to fulfill our God-given purpose. He does not want us to have the abundant life that God intends for us to have, as stated in His Word, "The thief cometh not, but for to steal, and to kill, and to destroy: I am come that they might have life, and that they might have it more abundantly" (John 10:10).

Hence, the devil has a number of devices, tricks, and moves that he uses to distract, detour, delay, and if we allow him, even destroy our ability to accomplish our goals.

Well, without a doubt, the devil can be beat at his own game! The victory is ours! Who has possession of the ball? The Word tells us that we have the authority, even the power that God has given us! Hence, we have possession of the ball.

The devil only has the control that we give him! Stop giving the devil control of the ball! Stop running from the devil, and start running the devil! It is time that we take an offensive approach!

Throughout history, men have sought to understand life. It has been described figuratively through simile, personification, metaphor and analogy. This book depicts life as a game.

Life is indeed a game of sorts, and with any game you have the following: Objective, Rules, Players, and Strategies. We must understand how the game works, even the various aspects of the game, in order to win.

Objective

Our objective is to win, to be victorious. Whether we realize it or not, we already have the victory, for the Word assures us, "Nay, in all these things we are more than conquerors through him that loved us" (Romans 8:37).

The end result, even the final outcome, is already known. In the Revelation of Jesus Christ to John, it is revealed to us how the story will end. We receive insight into the end times!

The end is simple…the devil loses, God wins! End of story! The question is *how* we manage…*how* we go through in order to get to…*how* we endure, for indeed we know "that the race is not to the swift, nor the battle to the strong" (Ecclesiastes 9:11) but to those who endure!

The devil's objective is to prevent us from enduring. He does whatever he can to try to get us to give up. Yet, we cannot give up; we cannot give in; and we cannot give out, for we already have the victory!

Who would quit and throw in the towel when the

victory is already assured? The question is not *will* we win? The question is how do we endure whilst we are here on this earth, whilst we are waiting?

Each day we go into battle (spiritual warfare). We need to be prepared and equipped. This manual will help us to practically apply what God has decreed in his Word to ensure that we are equipped to beat the devil at his own game!

> **The devil's objective is to prevent us from enduring.**

Rules

What are the rules of this game that we call life? There are no rules. Anything goes! The devil does not play fair! No one is off limits! Indeed we wonder about the loss of innocent babies, children being molested, elderly being murdered, and the many other horrible things that occur in this life. They seem to go against the rules, but we must realize that indeed we are in a war, and it is a spiritual war.

"For we wrestle not against flesh and blood, but against principalities, against powers, against the rulers of the darkness of this world, against spiritual wickedness in high places" (Ephesians 6:12).

But do we realize that we have the upper hand? We have been given "tools" that we can use, but we are choosing not to use them. Why are we choosing to do things the hard way?

If we need to dig a hole and we have a shovel, why would we use our hands instead of the shovel? Similarly, why would we not use the "tools" that God has equipped us with to beat the enemy at his own game?

Players

Who are the players? The players include us, the devil and his demons, everybody we encounter in life, and the Godhead, for indeed the Father allows the devil to "try" us (Job 1:6–12); the Son intercedes on our behalf (Romans 8:34); the Holy Spirit leads, guides, and directs us in the way of righteousness (Romans 8:4–14).

Strategies

This manual details ten ways that we, as Christians, can beat the devil at his own destructive, deceitful game. If we are constantly mindful of these biblical principles and utilize them in our daily lives, we are ensured success at beating the devil at his own game, hence fulfilling our God-given purposes in life, while obtaining everything that God has for us!

Premise

The premise of this book is that the reader is saved. Indeed the truth is hid from the unbeliever. "But if our gospel be hid, it is hid to them that are lost" (II Corinthians 4:3). If you don't know Jesus Christ as Lord and Savior of your life, stop now and receive the plan of salvation. Repeat the following: Dear Lord, please forgive me for my sins. I am ready to surrender all and give my life to you. I believe that you became flesh and were born of the Virgin Mary, that you died on the cross for my sins, and that you rose again the third day with all power. According to Your Word, dear God, in Romans 10:9, I believe "That if thou shalt confess with thy mouth the Lord Jesus, and shalt believe in thine heart that God hath raised him from the dead, thou shalt be saved." On this day, dear God, I thank you for saving me and becoming Lord and Savior of my life.

10 Ways to Beat the Devil at His Own Game

1 Preventive Prayer

2 Constant, Continual Prayer

3 Intercessory Prayer

4 Fasting

5 Tithing

6 Praise and Thanksgiving

7 Knowledge of the Word

8 Trusting God

9 Seeking First the Kingdom of God

10 Being Aware of the Snares of the Enemy

Prayer...

What is prayer? Prayer is an address or petition to God. It provides a direct line of access to the Father.

Since we are able to go boldly to the throne for ourselves, we have access to the Father, through the Son. "Therefore come boldly unto the throne of grace, that we may obtain mercy, and find grace to help in time of need" (Hebrews 4:16).

We can never underestimate the power of prayer. Prayer truly does change things! In II Chronicles 7:1–15, we find Solomon closing his prayer, which is followed by fire coming down from heaven and the glory of the Lord filling the house. In verse 12, the Lord appeared to Solomon and said, "I have heard thy prayer, and have chosen this place to myself for a house of sacrifice." In verse 15, the Lord says, "Now mine eyes shall be open, and mine ears attent unto the prayer that is made in this place."

As the aforementioned scriptures indicate, prayer is a powerful and essential tool in the hands of the believer. This is re-iterated throughout God's holy Word. If we are to be equipped in beating the devil at his own game, we must utilize the power of prayer!

In II Chronicles 7:14, God, through his man-servant Ezra, tells us that "If my people, which are called by my name, shall humble themselves, and pray, and seek my face, and turn from their wicked ways; then will I hear from heaven, and will forgive their sin, and will heal their land."

This manual looks at three distinct types of prayer: preventive prayer, continual prayer, and intercessory prayer.

Preventive Prayer

Many times we find ourselves turning to God when troubling or difficult times beset us. Although there is nothing wrong with turning to God during those times, it is also essential that we realize the power of preventive prayer.

Preventive means to keep from happening or existing. We are able to keep anticipated hostile action from happening, even able to hinder it and altogether stop it. Hence, it is indeed good that we begin our day with prayer.

Not a morning passes without my husband leading us in prayer before the children leave to go to school or we leave to go to work. It is a way to ensure that we are all focused as the day begins. It ensures that the last communication amongst us before returning home is a positive word of prayer. It shows that we value prayer and realize the power that it has. It shows that we consider God to be an essential part of our family and would not dare think of starting the day without talking to Him.

When we engage in preventive prayer, we are

unleashing the power of the Holy Spirit to lead, guide, and direct our lives. We are saying that we realize that we are not in control of ourselves, for we have given that control to the Holy Spirit. We are covering ourselves and getting prepared for whatever we may face when we equip ourselves through preventive prayer.

When we pray about things in advance, we open up the communication lines with God. We stop many of the plans the devil may have had right in their tracks. We hinder, impede, and altogether prevent many of the darts that the enemy has planned to throw our way.

Instead of being hit by a dart, preventive prayer keeps the dart from even being formed or thrown. The Bible instructs us to always watch and pray. "Watch ye therefore, and pray always, that ye may be accounted worthy to escape all these things that shall come to pass, and to stand before the Son of man" (Luke 21:36).

> **Instead of being hit by a dart, preventive prayer keeps the dart from even being formed or thrown.**

In this game of life, preventive prayer is an essential element in beating the devil at his own game! We must take an offensive approach and take possession of the ball, which represents our lives, by utilizing and not overlooking the power of preventive prayer!

Constant, Continual Prayer

"Now when Daniel knew that the writing was signed, he went into his house; and his windows being open in his chamber toward Jerusalem, he kneeled upon his knees three times a day, and prayed, and gave thanks before his God, as he did aforetime" (Daniel 6:10).

Daniel prayed three times per day. When and how often should *we* pray?

I Thessalonians 5:17 "Pray without ceasing."

Colossians 4:2 "Continue in prayer…"

Ephesians 6:18 "Praying always with all prayer and supplication in the Spirit…"

As the scriptures indicate, we should constantly and continually pray. We should never let our guard down! We should always be in a state of prayer, meditation and praise.

We should constantly pray, not just when in turmoil. Prayer is so essential that in Matthew 6:5–13, Jesus gives us the Lord's Prayer in which he instructs us on how to pray.

Indeed, we must constantly and continually pray in

order to beat the devil at his own destructive game! For we know that there is power in prayer, that prayer truly changes things, even "...That if two of you shall agree on earth as touching any thing that they shall ask, it shall be done for them of my Father which is in heaven" (Matthew 18:19). Furthermore, we know that "...The effectual, fervent prayer of a righteous man availeth much" (James 5:16).

Can you imagine the difference in your life and the lives of those that you encounter if you are in a continual state of prayer as we are instructed in the Word of God? Can you not already see how the devil's antics will be limited if you are in this constant mode of prayer? Your responses, reactions, and interactions would all be tempered by this state of constant, continual prayer.

> **We should constantly pray, not just when in turmoil.**

Indeed, being in a state of constant, continual prayer will help ensure that you beat the devil at his own game!

Intercessory Prayer

Indeed we know the importance of and the difference that prayer can make in our lives. Do we not desire the same for others? If so, we need to intercede and pray for others.

The Bible says let the strong bear the infirmities of the weak! "We then that are strong ought to bear the infirmities of the weak, and not to please ourselves" (Romans 15:1). Hence, it is even our Christian responsibility to pray for others.

Indeed, we know that God hears the prayers of the saints. "And the smoke of the incense, which came with the prayers of the saints, ascended up before God out of the angel's hand" (Revelation 8:4). If we can "get a prayer through," we need to be praying for others.

Do we realize that many of us are saved today because somebody interceded and prayed for us? Somebody was willing to stand in the gap for us. Somebody, who recognized that we were lost in our sins and on our way to hell, interceded and prayed for us! There is indeed power in prayer!

"Peter therefore was kept in prison: but prayer was made without ceasing of the church unto God for him" (Acts 12:5).

Indeed, after Herod imprisoned Peter, the church interceded and prayed for him. The prayers of the righteous certainly did avail much! For the very night that Herod would have brought him forth, the Lord sent his angel and delivered him out of the prison, even out of the hand of Herod.

God does hear our prayer, and yes, God does still answer prayer! Prayer is an essential element in beating the devil at his own game.

> **Hence, it is even our Christian responsibility to pray for others.**

We can truly succeed in beating the devil at his own game if we utilize the power that God has given us through preventive prayer, constant, continual prayer, and intercessory prayer!

Fasting

Fasting is a practice that is often overlooked. It is imperative that we understand and utilize this as we embark on beating the devil at his own game.

In Matthew 17: 14–21, when the disciples ask Jesus why they were unable to cast out a demon, after admonishing them regarding their unbelief and lack of faith, Jesus says, "Howbeit this kind goeth not out but by prayer and fasting" (Matthew 17:21). It is evident that some things will occur *only* as a result of both prayer *and* fasting.

It is essential that we truly understand what fasting is if it is to be effective. Someone once said that if we "fast" without praying, then we are just starving. Fasting and praying go hand in hand.

Exactly what is fasting? Many consider it to be a form or method of prayer. They consider it to be self-denial, a sacrifice, and a way to break strongholds.

Fasting is indeed all of the above. It encompasses the aforementioned definitions. When we deny ourselves something we enjoy, we are sacrificing and showing God that we are willing to give up something that is important to us. We are reminded of Abraham's willingness to sacrifice his son Isaac (Genesis 22), and indeed God gave his only son, Jesus, to die for our sins. "For God so loved the world, that he gave his only begotten Son, that whosoever believeth in him should not perish, but have everlasting life" (John 3:16).

God honors sacrifice and our willingness to give up something and will bless our willingness to do so. Fasting is indeed a way of glorifying God.

There are many instances in the Bible when fasting was utilized, both individually and corporately. In the Bible, fasting was used prior to ordaining elders and commissioning apostles, interceding for God's people, humbling one's self, seeking God's will, seeking healing, petitioning God to withhold his judgment, and protection.

We are reminded of Esther, who instructed the people to join her in a period of fasting (Esther 4:16). She wanted to stop the devil in his tracks and prevent him from committing genocide and exterminating her people. Indeed, we know that the devil was stopped in his tracks.

Even with that, many people still do not see the need to fast. Yet Jesus even made it clear that the day would come for fasting. "Jesus said unto them, Can the children of the bridechamber mourn, as long as the bridegroom is with them? but the days will come, when the bridegroom shall be taken from them, and then shall they fast" (Matthew 9:15).

That day has come! As we look at beating the devil at his own game, in this game of life, when we utilize the practice of fasting, we further equip ourselves.

Indeed, we can pray about all things, but as Jesus said, some things only come through prayer *and* fasting! Let us use this offensive technique and defeat the devil at his own game!

> **Some things only come through prayer and fasting!**

Tithing

If we are serious about beating the devil at his own game, we cannot overlook the power of the tithe.

In the Old Testament book of Malachi, we find expressed the power that we have if we tithe.

Malachi 3:10–11 states:

> Bring ye all the tithes into the storehouse, that there may be meat in mine house, and prove me now herewith, saith the LORD of hosts, if I will not open you the windows of heaven, and pour you out a blessing, that there shall not be room enough to receive it. And I will rebuke the devourer for your sakes, and he shall not destroy the fruits of your ground; neither shall your vine cast her fruit before the time in the field, saith the LORD of hosts.

Many have been deceived by the great deceiver into believing that tithing is just an Old Testament principle that no longer applies, but Jesus says, in the New Testament, that He came not to destroy but to fulfill the law! "Think not that I am come to destroy the law, or the prophets: I am not come to destroy, but to fulfill" (Matthew 5:17).

If we truly want to tie the devil's hands and even handicap him, we must understand that we limit what he can do when we are tithers. We tithe out of obedience, and obedience is better than sacrifice (I Samuel 15:22). Indeed we protect our finances from the devil when we tithe.

If we really want to beat the devil at the game, we must be committed tithers, for God promises us in so doing that he will pour us out a blessing that we shall not have room enough to receive it! By tithing, we protect our finances, keeping them out of the reach of the enemy! Without a doubt, no weapon formed against us shall prosper (Isaiah 54:17).

It is astounding how many people do not truly understand tithing. Questions are continually posed regarding the issue. Unfortunately, the devil has used this as a way to trick and deceive many.

There are some churches that talk about "being a 5% tither" (which is in itself an oxymoron!), even telling people they can choose to tithe from their net or gross, and many are fearful of discussing the tithe at all.

But how can we be afraid to say what the Word of God says?

As indicated in the following scriptures, the Word instructs us to tithe:

Leviticus 27:30 "And all the tithe of the land, whether of the seed of the land, or of the fruit of the tree, is the Lord's: it is holy unto the Lord."

Deuteronomy 14:22 "Thou shalt truly tithe all the increase of they seed, that the field bringeth forth year by year."

Exodus 23:19 "The first of the first fruits of thy land thou shalt bring into the house of the Lord thy God..."

The Word tells us that the tithe is the tenth:

Leviticus 27:32 "And concerning the tithe of the herd, or of the flock, even of whatsoever passeth under the rod, the tenth shall be holy unto the Lord."

The Word tells us that we are to tithe from our increase:

Proverbs 3:9–10 "Honor the Lord with thy substance, and with the first fruits of all thine increase: So shall thy barns be filled with plenty, and thy presses shall burst out with new wine."

Indeed, it is not negotiable and cannot be compromised!

If we are not tithing, as directed by the Word of

God, we are not fully equipped to beat the devil at his own game!

> **Many have been deceived by the great deceiver into believing that tithing is just an Old Testament principle.**

Even in my personal life, I am a true witness that tithing works! I have experienced God's blessings in my finances over and over and over again! Since I became a true tither, my life has never been the same! It is evident that God has indeed rebuked the devourer for my sake. Because of my obedience, I am even experiencing God's favor! And God's favor is better than money in the bank…which tithing can give you!

Praise and Thanksgiving

Praise opens the floodgates of heaven! Indeed, when the praises go up, the blessings come down! We must praise God in season and out of season, during good times and bad times! We should wake up with praise on our lips and lie down with praise in our hearts.

"This shall be written for the generation to come: and the people which shall be created shall praise the Lord" (Psalm 102:18).

We truly steal the ball from the devil when we do what we were created to do, regardless of situations, circumstances, or adversities, and praise God! We must learn to thank God for all things, even the little things. If we are not truly thankful for the little things, how can we expect God to bless us with bigger things?

When we learn to praise God and be thankful for even the little things, we are able to beat the devil at his own game of trying to distress and even depress us by causing us to focus on what we do not have. The songwriter said that not only is praise what I do, but praise is who I am! I would not have the rocks to cry out for me, for He is worthy even of the highest praise, Hallelujah!

In Philippians 4:11 Paul says, "Not that I speak in respect of want: for I have learned, in whatsoever state I am, therewith to be content." We, too, should be content and thankful for all that God has done for us, instead of focusing on what we do not have. If we spend more time praising God and thanking Him for what we have, we will not always be concerned about what we don't have.

We can beat the devil at his own game if we spend more time praising and thanking God for all he has done and continues to do for us. If we focus on that, we won't have time to worry about what we do not have. This ties the hands of the enemy who wants us in bondage and worry. "But my God shall supply all your need according to his riches in glory by Christ Jesus" (Philippians 4:19). Indeed, God has promised us that he will provide all of our needs, according to His riches in glory.

In the Word of God, we are even commanded to praise God. *It is not optional!* If we spend more time giving God the praise and thanksgiving He is due, we will be further equipped to beat the devil at his own game!

The enemy wants to steal our focus. He wants to take our focus off of God, but we cannot allow that to happen! When we are praising and thanking God, our focus is where it needs to be—on God! For it is not about us anyway! It is all about Jesus!

As long as we keep our focus where it belongs—on Jesus—we are further equipped at beating the devil at his own game!

> **If we are not truly thankful for the little things, how can we expect God to bless us with bigger things?**

Knowledge of the Word

"As newborn babes, desire the sincere milk of the word, that ye may grow thereby" (I Peter 2:2).

It is essential that we spend time in the Word!

We must "Study to show thyself approved unto God, a workman that needeth not to be ashamed, rightly dividing the word of truth" (II Timothy 2:15).

The Word is essential in defeating the enemy. This great fact and lesson is demonstrated when the tempter comes to Jesus in the wilderness. Jesus fights with the Word. Jesus responds to the devil with the Word (Matthew 4:1–11).

How can we hope to withstand the wiles of the enemy if we do not know God's holy Word? How can the Word be brought back to our remembrance if we do not know it, if we have not spent time studying and meditating on it?

It has been said that the Word contains an answer to anything and everything that we encounter in life. It has been termed our road map. How can we expect to know how to handle life's situations and circumstances if we do not know how the Word directs us to handle them?

Indeed, when Jesus left this world, He said that He would not leave us comfortless. "…and, lo, I am with you alway, even unto the end of the world" (Matthew 28:20). Not only did He send the Holy Spirit, but God has given us his Word via the Holy Bible.

What we need to live by is contained in God's book, the Bible. *I do not know about you, but when I stand before God at the Judgment Seat of Christ, I want to be able to say, "I read your book! I took time out of the life that you gave me to read your book!"*

We must remember that "the weapons of our warfare are not carnal, but mighty through God to the pulling down of strongholds" (II Corinthians 10:4), and "Thy word is a lamp unto my feet, and a light unto my path" (Psalm 119:105). Indeed, the Word is the sword of the Spirit (Ephesians 6:17).

The importance of knowing, adhering to, and obeying the Word of God is essential. Jesus said, "For whosoever shall do the will of my Father which is in heaven, the same is my brother, and sister, and mother" (Matthew 12:50).

We must spend time with the Word of God! It is imperative that we feed our spirits; just as we need to feed our physical bodies to live, we need to feed our "spirit man" to flourish.

Indeed, the enemy does not want us to be equipped, to be strong from the Word, so he constantly tries to distract us from the Word of God. What is consuming your time and causing you not to spend more time in God's Word? Examine anything that keeps you from reading God's Word to see if it is a tool of the devil.

We should not ever be *too* busy for God's Word! In order to be equipped to beat the devil at his own game, we must spend time reading, studying, and meditating on God's Holy Word! We can beat the devil at his own destructive game if we equip ourselves with the Word of God—for it is our sword, and with it, we can fight all battles!

> **What is consuming your time and causing you not to spend more time in God's Word?**

Trusting God

In whom should we put our trust, our assured reliance?

"It is better to trust in the Lord than to put confidence in man" (Psalm 118:8).

In order to be fully equipped to beat the devil at his own destructive game, we must trust God totally, completely, unconditionally! Trusting God is not optional! It is essential!

"Trust in the Lord with all thine heart, and lean not unto thine own understanding. In all thy ways acknowledge him, and he shall direct thy paths" (Proverbs 3:5–6).

We must trust God, no matter what, at all times, and in all things! Furthermore, Psalm 37:3–5 states, "Trust in the Lord, and do good; so shalt thou dwell in the land, and verily thou shalt be fed. Delight thyself also in the Lord; and he shall give thee the desires of thine heart. Commit thy way unto the Lord; trust also in him; and he shall bring it to pass." Indeed, there are even some promises attached to trusting God.

Many people only want to trust God when it is convenient for them, when things are going the way that they want. However, that is not enough. We must learn to trust God even when things "look" dreary, even when things don't "seem" or "appear" to be going our way.

If we truly trust God, we are not disturbed or even dismayed at things that occur, for we know that God is in control. We trust that God is directing our paths. We know that God wants what is best for us. We know, even, that there is a reason for everything. We even know that we do not go through difficult times or adversity alone, for we have the Holy Spirit.

When we truly realize that, as the Word says in Romans 8:28, "And we know that all things work together for good to them that love God, to them who are the called according to his purpose," then we are able to completely trust God! We will not find ourselves distressed or dismayed at life's turns, for we have confidence, as Christians, that whatever happens, somehow, someway, even by the grace of God, that it is working for our good! For we know that God is in total control!

Even when certain things are taken away from us, we must still continue to trust God. Many times we are guilty of trying to hold on to things, such as vehicles, houses, jobs, and people, even to unhealthy relationships. However, at times, things and people have to be removed from our lives in order for us to obtain what God has for us!

Have we ever been guilty of trying to hold on to a relationship…only to have it end and have God to bless us with the "right" mate for us? Have we ever been guilty of trying to hold on to a vehicle, house, or even a job…only to have God to bless us with an even better vehicle, house, or job?

Joseph realized, as he comforted his brothers after the death of their father, that although his brothers thought evil against him, "God meant it unto good, to bring to pass, as it is this day, to save much people alive" (Genesis 50:20).

We, too, must know that even though the devil means it for bad, God means it for our good! God is in control, and what God has for us, it is for us!

When we truly realize, as Christians, that *all* things work together for our good, and when we learn to trust God completely, we will be further equipped at beating the devil at his own game!

When we trust God, the enemy is rendered impotent, and there is nothing he can do to penetrate, for we know, without a doubt, that God is in control!

> **We must trust God totally, completely, unconditionally!**

9

Seeking First the Kingdom of God

If we desire to truly be equipped at beating the devil at his own game, without a doubt, we must seek first the kingdom of God and His righteousness.

"But seek ye first the kingdom of God, and his righteousness; and all these things shall be added unto you" (Matthew 6:33).

Righteousness refers to living according to the Word of God. This is a command. It is an order. It is not optional. Many have been deceived into thinking this a one-time seeking occurring at salvation. However, it should be a constant, continual seeking.

We should make sure that always and ever-present in our spirit is that of seeking first the kingdom of God and His righteousness. When that is our focus, we do not have time for anything else! When that is our focus, we do not have to worry about being distracted or deceived by the enemy. We are to strive to live a righteous, holy life at all times, in all ways.

We have to realize that we are representing Jesus

Christ, that we are witnesses. As Christians, bearing the name of Jesus Christ, we have a responsibility to represent Him well. Not only does the Word instruct us to seek first the kingdom of God and His righteousness, but the Word even tells us how to succeed in fulfilling this command.

Just to name a few, we can be sure that we are seeking first the kingdom of God and His righteousness by: Walking in love (Ephesians 5:1–2), being filled with the Spirit (Ephesians 5:18–21), thinking on certain things (Philippians 4:8), holy living (I Peter 1:13–16), and being a hearer and a doer of the Word (James 1:19–22).

> **Many have been deceived into thinking this a one-time seeking occurring at salvation.**

Without a doubt, if we want to be further equipped at beating the devil at his own destructive game, we must constantly and continually seek first the kingdom of God and His righteousness.

10

Being Aware of the Snares of the Enemy

We must get to a point that we can recognize the enemy! For according to I Peter 5:8, "Your adversary the devil, as a roaring lion, walketh about, seeking whom he may devour." Furthermore, in John 10:10 the Bible says that "the thief cometh not, but for to steal, and to kill, and to destroy."

We have to be able to recognize when the devil is on the scene, when the devil is at work. He will come at us any way that he can. He will use our family members. He will use our friends. He will use our co-workers. He comes along when we are simply minding our own business. If we are not careful, we might not even see him coming!

For we know that according to Ephesians 6:12, "For we wrestle not against flesh and blood, but against principalities, against powers, against the rulers of the darkness of this world, against spiritual wickedness in high places."

In order to be equipped at beating the devil at his

game, we must be aware of his snares, his tricks, his devices. In other words, we must be able to recognize the enemy. A thorough examination of the Word of God will provide insight into the tools of the enemy. This manual will only deal with a few, namely doubt, deception and denial of the truth of God's Word.

If we ever find ourselves doubting, the victim or even the author of deception, or denying the truths of God's Word, then we are falling prey to the tools of the enemy. The devil is aware of how powerful we are as men and women of faith. Hence, he tries to get us to doubt.

Doubt is defined as a lack of confidence in; distrust; uncertainty of belief or opinion that often interferes with decision-making. Doubt is one of the enemy's primary tools. If he can get us to doubt, then he is able to defeat us in many areas and aspects of our lives.

If we doubt the power of prayer, then we will not pray. If we doubt the importance of fasting, then we will not fast. If we doubt the necessity of tithing, then we will not tithe.

> **We must get to a point that we can recognize the enemy!**

If we doubt the need to honor God with our praise and thanksgiving, then we will not have God as the center of our lives. If we doubt the importance of reading and studying the Word of God for ourselves, then we will not spend time in the Word. If we doubt that *all* things work together for our good and that God is in control, then we will not totally trust God. If we doubt that we need to seek first the kingdom of God and His righteousness, then our focus will not be where it should be—on Jesus.

Indeed, the enemy's tool of doubt can be extremely destructive in the lives of Christians. Doubt can serve to cancel out the promises and blessings of God for our lives. For throughout the Word, *by our faith* is reiterated. The woman with the issue of blood was healed *by her faith*. The dumb were able to speak *by faith*. The blind were able to see *by faith*.

Indeed, the Word says, "But without faith it is impossible to please him: for he that cometh to God must believe that he is, and that he is a rewarder of them that diligently seek him" (Hebrews 11:6). Furthermore, "If thou canst believe, all things are possible to him that believeth" (Mark 9:23).

Regardless of the situation or circumstance, we must not succumb to the enemy's tools of doubt and unbelief. We must simply stand on the promises of God and have *faith*…no matter what!

Another one of the enemy's tools is deception. This is used along with doubt to strengthen the enemy's hold.

The enemy has even been referred to as the author of deception.

Exactly what is deception? Deception is synonymous with trick, fraud, and double-dealing. Deception causes people to deny the truth of God's Word. It allows the enemy to have us bound. But the Word of God says, "And ye shall know the truth, and the truth shall make you free" (John 8:32).

What is truth? Well, according to John 14:6, not only is Jesus the way, but the Word also says, even Jesus himself says, that He is truth! Jesus is truth! Since the enemy seeks to deceive us, to keep us from knowing the truth, to keep us from knowing Jesus, he uses the tool of deception, which is the opposite of truth. This deception causes many to deny the truth of God's Word. As a result, many are doubting and are not experiencing the abundant life that God desires for us to have. "The thief cometh not, but for to steal, and to kill, and to destroy: I am come that they might have life, and that they might have it more abundantly" (John 10:10).

We can beat the devil at his own game if we refuse to allow him to deceive us into denying the truth of God's Word, for we are to believe every word that proceedeth out of the mouth of God! "…It is written, Man shall not live by bread alone, but by every word that proceedeth out of the mouth of God" (Matthew 4:4).

Indeed, when we are aware of the snares of the enemy, we are further equipped to beat the devil at his own destructive game!

Afterward

Having on the Whole Armor

Ephesians 6: 10–20 reads:

> ¹⁰Finally, my brethren, be strong in the Lord, and in the power of his might.
>
> ¹¹Put on the whole armor of God, that ye may be able to stand against the wiles of the devil.
>
> ¹²For we wrestle not against flesh and blood, but against principalities, against powers, against the rulers of the darkness of this world, against spiritual wickedness in high places.
>
> ¹³Wherefore take unto you the whole armor of God, that ye may be able to withstand in the evil day, and having done all, to stand.
>
> ¹⁴Stand therefore, having your loins girt about with truth, and having on the breastplate of righteousness;

[15]And your feet shod with the preparation of the gospel of peace;

[16]Above all, taking the shield of faith, wherewith ye shall be able to quench all the fiery darts of the wicked.

[17]And take the helmet of salvation, and the sword of the Spirit, which is the word of God:

[18]Praying always with all prayer and supplication in the Spirit, and watching thereunto with all perseverance and supplication for all saints;

[19]And for me, that utterance may be given unto me, that I may open my mouth boldly, to make known the mystery of the gospel,

[20]For which I am an ambassador in bonds: that therein I may speak boldly, as I ought to speak.

Indeed, the Bible makes it clear that we are to put on the whole armor of God, that we may be able to stand against the wiles of the devil.

The question has been posed: Can we fight without the whole armor, if a piece of the armor is missing? The answer is yes, for indeed, we do not have a choice about being in the battle, even being in warfare.

However, without the whole armor, we are vulnerable. Without the whole armor, we may receive some "wounds" that could have been prevented. This manual helps to ensure that we have on the whole armor at all times.

In briefly examining the armor, we note that *Truth* refers to the knowledge of the truth of God's Word, Tool #7 of the believer; the *Breastplate of Righteousness* refers to living a righteous, holy life, Tool #9 of the believer; *Preparation of the Gospel of Peace* refers to being ready and equipped to advance against the enemy with an offensive approach, the entire aim of this manual; the *Shield of Faith* refers to believing, and not doubting, every word that proceedeth out of the mouth of God, even standing on His promises, Tool #10 of the believer; the *Helmet of Salvation* refers to assurance of salvation, the premise of this manual; and the *Sword of the Spirit*, which is the Word of God, is indeed the foundation of this manual.

Without a doubt, we *can* have on the whole armor and we *can* beat the devil at his own destructive game!

In Conclusion...

Just as the armor is not as effective if a piece is missing, hence leaving us vulnerable and susceptible, the tools of the believer noted in this manual are only effective *if they are used*.

If we truly want to tear Satan's kingdom down, to beat the devil at his own game, we need to utilize our tools as believers of:

1. Preventive Prayer
2. Constant, Continual Prayer
3. Intercessory Prayer
4. Fasting
5. Tithing
6. Praise and Thanksgiving
7. Knowledge of the Word
8. Trusting God
9. Seeking First the Kingdom of God
10. Being Aware of the Snares of the Enemy